Evan Goodfellow

Photography by
Tadashi Yamaoda

Tricks performed by Evan Goodfellow
and friends

Tracks Publishing
San Diego, California

PUBLISHING

Cover photo: Bruce Tucker
Rider: Chris Kendall

Skateboarding: Ramp Tricks

Evan Goodfellow

PUBLISHING

Tracks Publishing
140 Brightwood Avenue
Chula Vista, CA 91910
619-476-7125
tracks@cox.net
www.startupsports.com

Publisher's Cataloging-in-Publication

    Goodfellow, Evan.
        Skateboarding : ramp tricks / Evan Goodfellow ; photography by Tadashi Yamaoda ; tricks performed by Evan Goodfellow and friends.
        p. cm.
        Includes index.
        SUMMARY: Instructional guide to learning skateboarding tricks on ramps. Explores thirty-five tricks in sequential photographs with captions. Also discusses the history of ramp skateboarding and includes biographies of influential riders.
        Audience: Ages 10-25.
        LCCN 2006903275
        ISBN 1-884654-26-6

        1. Skateboarding.   I. Title.

GV859.8.G659 2006   796.22
                        QBI06-200075

I dedicate this book
to my family and friends.
Thanks for encouraging
me to skateboard.

Acknowledgements

Thanks to

Tadashi Yamaoda for performing tricks and taking the photos.

Cody Branin for performing tricks.

Jim Montalbano for graphic production.

Phyllis Carter for editing.

Preface

Among the goals of this book is to give readers a little history of skateboarding as well as an appreciation for its current status. Ramps have played an important part in skateboarding and continue to do so. *Skateboarding: Ramp Tricks* attempts to equip the reader with a better understanding of how to ride ramps. We start out with basics and progressively explore more challenging tricks.

The introduction presents icons in ramp skateboarding including Tony Hawk, Bob Burnquist, Christian Hosoi and Gator. Most current skateboarding books do not discuss innovative skaters of past generations. Although young skateboarders may be unfamiliar with their names, it's important to take a brief look at the veterans who helped the sport evolve.

The great thing about ramps is that they are everywhere! With the recent popularization of skateboarding and in-line skating, more and more communities have built outdoor skateboard parks, which usually consist of halfpipes and various other ramps. This book will explain how to utilize properly the ramps at local skate parks.

The second part of the book breaks down each trick frame by frame so the reader can understand where his or her feet should be and how to position the body. Captions explain what the rider should be thinking before, during and after the trick. Through sequential photos and captions, readers will have the tools needed to expand their bag of tricks.

Contents

Intro

Ramp skateboarding has always defied the laws of gravity. Ramps allow skateboarders to get all four wheels off the ground. Ramps come in all shapes and sizes — from a jacked up piece of plywood, to somebody's empty swimming pool, to an elaborate halfpipe. They can be six inches or three stories high.

Ramp skateboarding has been pushed to new levels since its conception. Skateboarders continue to build bigger, steeper and crazier ramps in an attempt to break new ground and pull new tricks. Like ramps, ramp tricks have progressed and become more challenging over time. Today's everyday tricks would not have been considered just 10 years ago. The evolution of ramps and ramp tricks has created considerable excitement and nurtured mainstream attention, thus helping to establish the legitimacy of skateboarding as a sport, not a fad.

Dogtown and the Z-Boys

The beginning of ramp skating took place in the mid '70s with skateboard legends Stacey Peralta, Tony Alva, Jay Adams and other members of the Dogtown crew. These individuals grew up in the Santa Monica, California area known as Dogtown. They were surfer kids who put surfing moves into skateboarding.

They took their boards to schoolyards and developed turns and carves on the cement and asphalt banks. As their ability

11

> **Every new, crazy trick was something that had never been done before.**

increased, they sought more challenging terrain. The crew began jumping over fences and skating drained swimming pools. At this time there was a drought in California and pool owners were ordered not to fill their pools. This provided ample opportunity for the Dogtown crew to begin experimenting. If the folks were not home, over the wall and into the bowl the skaters went.

Each session was an attempt to do something new on a skateboard. Every new, crazy trick was something that had never been done before. Stacey Peralta says that skateboarders who came after the Dogtown crew were fortunate to know whether a certain trick was possible. During the Dogtown days, if a trick had never been done before, they had no way of knowing whether it was possible until they landed it.

Many of the Dogtown crew members went on to start their own skate teams and companies and continued to be an influence in the skateboard industry. In 1979 Stacey Peralta gathered a bunch of up-and-coming skaters and built a team that changed the sport forever. This team was called the Bones Brigade, and one of the riders was Tony Hawk. You may have heard of him.

The Bones Brigade skated for Powell Peralta. Powell Peralta was owned by George Powell and Stacey Peralta. Many of the riders who rode for the Bones Brigade were hand selected by Stacey. This skateboard team was famous for its innovative tricks, contest winnings and, most importantly, videos.

Powell Peralta

Number	Title	Date
1	The Bones Brigade Video Show	1984
2	Future Primitive	1985
3	The Search for Animal Chin	1987
4	Public Domain	1988
5	Axe Rated	1988
6	Ban This	1989
7	Propaganda	1990
8	Eight	1991
9	Celebrity Tropical Fish	1991

Powell

10	Hot Batch	1992
11	Chaos	1992
12	Play	1993
13	Suburban Diners	1994
14	Scenic Drive	1995
15	Strip Mall Heroes	1998
16	Magic	1999
17	Bones Bearings Class of 2000	1999

Although other skateboard companies were making videos at the time, none compared in terms of skateboarding talent, quality and story line. The most notable video was *The Search for Animal Chin*. It features the Bones Brigade Team in a fiction plot seeking the founder of skateboarding. The founder is named Animal Chin who dates back to the time

of Confucius. The team tours the world in search of Animal Chin to get back to the roots of skateboarding and to escape commercial hype. The video ends with the riders finding and riding a complex system of halfpipes that are all connected to each other.

A roster of the early Bones Brigade riders:

Blair Arnot
Ray Barbee
Chris Borst
Pat Brennen
Steve Caballero
Adrian Demain
Alan Gelfand
Tommy Guerrero
Kevin Harris
Tony Hawk
Frankie Hill
Bucky Lasek
Mike McGill
Colin McKay
Lance Mountain
Rodney Mullen
Ray Rodriguez
Steve Saiz
Chris Senn
Steve Steadham
Jim Thiebaud
Chet Thomas
Ray Underhill
Mike Vallely
Danny Way
Per Welinder

http://en.wikipedia.org/wiki/Bones_Brigade

Many of these pros continue to be great influences in skateboarding. Steve Caballero still rides for Powell and has celebrated his 25th year riding for the team. Ray Barbee rides for the Firm, which was started by Bones Brigader Lance Mountain. Tony Hawk and Per Welinder went on to form Birdhouse Projects, which is one of the most successful skateboard companies in the world. Collin McKay and Danny Way built DC Shoes from humble beginnings into a major skateboard shoe company. Chet Thomas continues to ride professionally and has successfully reinvented himself to keep up with the changes of the sport.

Mark "Gator" Ragowski

Mark Anthony Rogowski was born in 1966 in Brooklyn, New York. In the early '70s he moved with his older brother and mother to Escondido, California. In 1979 Gator made his first appearance on the skateboarding scene when he won a major amateur skateboard contest in Canada. In 1982-83 he began to collect sponsors that included Gullwing Trucks and Vans Shoes. Five years later, Gator won an important event called the Del Mar National Contest. After winning this contest he turned pro for Vision Skateboards. SkateVision released a video that featured Gator's amazing abilities. The performance elevated him to celebrity status.

Vision Skateboards had its own line of clothing called Vision Street Wear, which was very popular among skateboarders and non-skateboarders alike. Gator was awarded his own clothing line. He graced the cover of all the skate mags and continued to win or place in many contests. In the mid-1980s Gator had pro spotlights in the two big skate magazines, *Transworld Skateboarding* and *Thrasher*. He was continuously approached for sponsorship deals and demos. He hired an agent to keep from going crazy. It was a big change from being a grubby little skateboard kid rolling around at the park to being a celeb. One demo Gator did for Swatch attracted more than 10,000 spectators.

Gator's skateboarding skills were phenomenal. His specialties were vert ramp and bowl skating. Gator could do long boardslides around bowl corners and get huge air over the coping. His runs could last for more than five minutes. He would stop only to catch his breath. He never missed a trick. His skating was always in control and cutting edge.

But things did not remain all glitz and glamour for Gator. He was unable to handle the fame and became arrogant and careless. At this time, vert skateboarding began taking a back seat to street skateboarding. Magazines and spectators showed a growing interest in curb tricks and freestyle street skating.

> *His [Gator's] skating was always in control and cutting edge.*

Gator's demise did not end with car accidents and arrests. He committed a murder and is serving 31 years in prison. Fortunately, his case is unique among legendary skate pros. Most kept out of trouble and found skateboarding to be a positive force in their lives.

Christian Hosoi

Christian Hosoi (Holmes) was born October 5, 1967. At the age of 5 he began skateboarding with Dogtown legends Shogo Kubo, Tony Alva, Stacey Peralta and Jay Adams. He grew up in the Venice Beach area where his style and skills were shaped. Christian was sponsored in the early '80s and his career took off.

His first sponsors were Dogtown Skates and Jimmy Z. Hosoi's glory days coincided with skateboarding's new popularity. Movies such as *Thrashing* and *Gleaming the Cube* capitalized on skating's raw image. Sponsors were paying big money for athletes to represent their products and both were featured in magazines nationwide. Hosoi's bank account overflowed from contest winnings and sponsorships.

Hosoi competed with top pros like Steve Caballero, Tony

Hawk, Natas Kaupas and Jeff Kendall. Many say that Tony Hawk's main competitor back then was Hosoi. Hosoi carved his fame through his legendary trick invention, the "Christ Air." Hosoi would get air on the vert ramp, and as he ascended, he would kick the board into his hand and make the shape of the cross with his body. As he descended he would place his board back under his feet and ride back into the ramp. Hosoi was legendary for the height he achieved above the top of the ramp.

Hosoi, like many other pros at that time, thought the money would never end. But a recession hit the sport in the early 1990s, and Hosoi found himself struggling to make ends meet. After changing sponsors several times, he disappeared from the skateboard scene. In 2000 Hosoi was charged with drug trafficking and sent to prison for four years. Since then Hosoi has reexamined his life and taken some positive steps. He has reemerged on the skateboard scene with Quicksilver and other sponsors.

Tony Hawk

Tony Hawk is the face of pro skateboarding. Tony has spent his entire life and career pioneering the sport and ramp riding in particular. He became famous at a young age, continued as a pro skateboarder well into his 30s and is still at it today. He is hugely popular and especially so with young riders. Kids love Tony Hawk because he loves skateboarding.

Tony Hawk was born May 12, 1968 in Carlsbad, California. His first sponsor was with Powell Peralta's elite Bones Brigade. Tony's first photos in magazines show a skinny, long-haired blond kid catching air four times his height. Tony Hawk turned pro at 16. His sponsors included Airwalk Shoes.

In the early 1980s it was very difficult to turn pro. It was even more difficult to do so for elite companies like Powell and Airwalk. At the time there were two pros who had a pro model shoe, Natas Kapas for Etnies and Steve Caballero for Vans. Tony Hawk was only the third pro skateboarder to receive a pro model shoe in his name.

Many pro skateboarders came from broken homes or had parents who didn't take an interest in the sport. Tony Hawk's family was an exception. He had a very supportive father who found a way to get involved in his son's life and passion. Frank Hawk was instrumental in making skateboarding a legitimate sport, helped found the National Skateboard Association and actively supported early skateboard contests. He also helped build Tony's first halfpipe.

Tony Hawk is synonymous with skateboarding for good reason. He created many new tricks in vert skateboarding and is well known for the way he turns. In 1985 Tony Hawk landed his first 720, which is a spin of two revolutions. In 1999 he completed the most revolutions ever — a 900 — a spin of two and a half revolutions. He performed it at the 1999 X Games after failing 11 times. This trick won him first place and, of course, the skate world went crazy.

In 1999 Tony Hawk's status soared even higher with the release of his video game, *Tony Hawk's Pro Skater*. There have been seven sequels all meeting with great success. The video games include *Tony Hawk's Pro Skater 2, Tony Hawk's Pro Skater 3, Tony Hawk's Pro Skater 4, Tony Hawk's Underground 1* and *2, Tony Hawk's Underground 2 Remix* and *Tony Hawk's American Wasteland*.

In 2000 Tony wrote his autobiography, *Hawk: Occupation: Skateboarder,* which made *The New York Times* best-seller list. He has also written *Hawk* and another book titled *Between Boardslides and Burnout*, which is a road journal.

In January 1992 Tony Hawk and Per Welinder created the

Kids love Tony Hawk because he loves skateboarding.

skateboard company, Birdhouse Projects. The company produces quality products as well as featuring a top ranked team. His business ventures include Adio Shoes and Hawk Clothing.

Tony Hawk has been featured in numerous commercials, TV shows and movies. He has appeared in commercials for Apple Computer and Domino's Pizza. He has appeared in *Cyberchase, Rocket Power, The Simpsons, Max Steel, Sifl and Olly* and *CSI: Miami*. His movies include *Jackass: The Movie, The New Guy, Haggard, Max Keeble's Big Movie* and *Dogtown and Z-Boys*. He also has had acting parts in *Gleaming the Cube* and *Police Academy 4*.

http://en.wikipedia.org/wiki/Tony_Hawk

Steve Caballero

Steve Caballero was born November 8, 1964 in San Jose, California. He is a dedicated and committed skater who has been a positive agent of change. He started skating when he was 12 and was sponsored a year later by a skate park. In 1978 at the age of 15, Steve was sponsored by Powell Peralta. In 1980 Steve turned pro during the Gold Cup series at a Southern California contest.

Over the years Steve has collected many sponsors including Vans Shoes. He had a signature model shoe in the early '80s. In an interview with *Thrasher,* he was asked why he didn't start his own skateboard company like other top pros. He said other pros had to start their own companies due to not-so-generous skateboard sponsor checks. He was able to devote his time to skating because of the money he got from his shoe deal with Vans.

> *He [Steve] is a dedicated and committed skater who has been a positive agent of change.*

Steve has invented a slew of tricks — tricks that are now commonplace in both ramp and street skateboarding. Among the most notable are the Caballerial and the half cab. He invented both tricks while riding a vert bowl. The Caballerial was invented around 1980 in the 10-foot keyhole pool at Winchester Skateboard Park. The Caballerial is when you ride fakie and do a fakie 360 ollie. The half cab is a variation of this trick, but you turn 180 instead of 360. The frontside rock n roll slide, now usually called a frontside boardslide, is another of Steve's inventions.

Although Steve Caballero first became famous for his ramp skating, including launch ramps, bowls and vert, he was able to keep up when the focus changed to street. When asked if he found it easy to change from ramps to street, he said he found it very difficult. He said that he had always found skateboarding to be hard. But that was one of the reasons he found skating to be so exciting. He always felt challenged.

While some of the early pros got caught up with fame and fortune, Steve kept a level head. He practices Zen Buddhism and abstinence from drugs and alcohol. Steve Cabellero also enjoys being in a punk band, painting and motocross.

http://en.wikipedia.org/wiki/Steve_Caballero

http://secure.thrashermagazine.com/index.php?SCREEN=interview_cab&page_num=1

Colin McKay

Colin McKay was born August 29, 1975 in Vancouver, B.C., Canada. He first made his appearance on the skateboard scene in the Powell Peralta video, *Public Domain*. He grew up skating in the famous skateboard parks of Vancouver. He learned how to ride vert ramps at the Richmond Skate Ranch. He skated with pros like Sluggo, Moses Itkonen and Rick Howard. Colin McKay was younger than many of the other vert riders. He was envied for his youth and amazing ability, which was comparable to other pros twice his age.

After riding for Powell, many of his teammates were moving on and starting their own companies. As Powell began to break up, Colin made the switch to the new up-and-coming company, Plan B. Many of the Bones Brigade members had chosen Plan B including Danny Way and Rodney Mullen.

Skateboarders around the world began to notice Colin McKay during his stint with Plan B. His diverse skating was demonstrated in Plan B's *Virtual Reality* video. In this video Colin showed that he was not only an amazing vert skater but also an accomplished street skater. This combination of skills is highly unusual.

Colin took his street tricks and applied them to vert. His tricks include the switch 360 flip, switch backside heelflip noseslide, and the most impressive, nollie flip backside tailslide revert. His overwhelming tricks, contest results and video parts helped launch Colin to a place of influence in the skateboard industry. Colin was instrumental in lifting vert skating to a place of prominence in modern skateboarding. Colin still skates professionally and has business interests in several companies including Red Dragons Skate Supply, DC Shoes and Plan B.

Bob Burnquist

Bob Burnquist was raised in Sao Paulo, Brazil. He began skateboarding at the age of 11 and turned pro at 14. At that time vert skateboarding was very big in Brazil and the contests intense. Only one skateboarder competed at a time while a panel of experts judged. This pressure to perform equipped Bob mentally for future contests.

In 1995 Bob Burnquist traveled to Vancouver, B.C. and competed in Slam City Jam, which is one of the largest pro contests in North America. Bob was virtually unknown on the pro circuit in North America. His runs were very complex and technical. Those watching had a hard time distinguishing what was switch stance and what was regular. Bob placed first at the contest and also won a few big-name sponsors. Bob's contest run in Vancouver received the highest score any vert skater had ever received in the history of pro skateboarding.

Bob Burnquist was instrumental in revitalizing vert skating in the late 1990s. In general, vert held little interest for most skaters (notable exceptions were Colin McKay, Tony Hawk and Danny Way). Bob is one of today's top vert pros. His sponsors include Activision, Hurley Clothing, Oakley, Nixon, Pro-Tec, The Firm Skateboards and Ricta. Bob Burnquist is a positive and powerful influence in skateboarding today.

Danny Way

Danny was born in 1974 in Portland, Oregon. He was rolling around on a skateboard at the age of 6 and frequented the Del Mar Skateboard Ranch, known for its cement bowls and gnarly vert ramps. By the age of 11 Danny had picked up two major sponsors, Hosoi and Vision. At 14 he was asked to ride for the famous Bones Brigade. He accepted, but after a few months, left the team to ride for H-Street, a famous skateboard company headed by Matt Hensley.

Danny was the first person to jump the Great Wall without the use of a motorized vehicle.

At the age of 17 Danny Way was awarded the prestigious Skater of the Year award by *Thrasher*. The magazine honors only one skater each year. It is very special to be selected due to the fierce competition in the world of skateboarding. Danny won the title again in 2004 becoming the only skateboarder to win the award twice.

Danny has suffered an array of injuries. In 1994 he broke his neck in a surfing accident. Between 1999 and 2002 he underwent seven surgeries — five on his knee and two on his shoulder. The night before his record-breaking jump in China, he fell during a practice jump. He tore a ligament and injured a bone in his foot. The foot was reportedly swollen to the size of a grapefruit, but Danny had his doctor inject a pain killer so that he could jump.

World records are Danny Way's specialties. In 1999 he achieved the largest recorded air — jumping out of a helicopter, making a 12-foot kickflip and landing in a vert ramp. In 2002 he conceived and built a gigantic ramp upon which he consequently set records for the longest jump, clearing 65 feet, and the highest air, 18 feet 3 inches. In 2003 he broke those records by jumping 75 feet and airing 23.5 feet above the top of the ramp. In 2004 he set a new long-distance record by jumping 79 feet while winning gold at the X Games in Los Angeles.

The most recent and greatest accomplishment of Danny Way's career took place in China in 2005. He constructed a $500,000 mega ramp up to the Great Wall of China. Jumping from this ramp was death defying. The drop in was more than six stories high. The gap he cleared was over 61 feet long. The speed reached after landing was 50 mph. Danny was the first person to jump the Great Wall without the use of a motorized vehicle. Most people would feel satisfied to have accomplished an eighth of what Danny has. But instead of sitting back and taking it easy, he promises that there is more to come.

Conclusion

Ramp skateboarding has and will always play an integral part in the sport of skateboarding. Through their fearlessness and creativity, ramp riders have propelled skateboarding to greater heights. Their accomplishments have in turn spurred ramp technology and construction. Just as Danny Way has created ramps to achieve the highest airs and longest jumps to date, we can expect greater ramps, bigger airs and longer jumps in the future. Many thanks to all the pros who have risked life and limb to set new standards and prove that skateboarding has no limits.

Sites:
www.wikipedia.org
www.dcshoes.com
www.dannyway.com
www.fhm.com
www.stokedmovie.com
www.bobburnquist.com
www.tonyhawk.com
www.expn.com
www.powellskateboards.com
www.z-boys.com

Ramp tricks

1. Drop in

1. Place your back foot squarely across the tail. Your front foot should be across the bolts of the front truck.
2. The tail should be resting on the coping with the back wheels snug against the ramp.

3. Place all your weight on your front foot as you begin the drop in.

4. Press your weight onto your front leg and push the wheels down to make contact with the ramp.

27

5. Throughout the drop in, it is important to lean forward so that your weight stays centered with the board.

6. Stay low to the board in order to keep your balance.

7. Most people do not lean forward enough and slip out causing pain to the buttocks.

Key to remember: This trick requires that you push all your weight onto your front foot. Hesitation will almost always result in falling. So just go for it!

2. Rock to fakie

1.Approach the coping with your back foot flat on the tail and your front foot across the bottom bolts of the top truck.

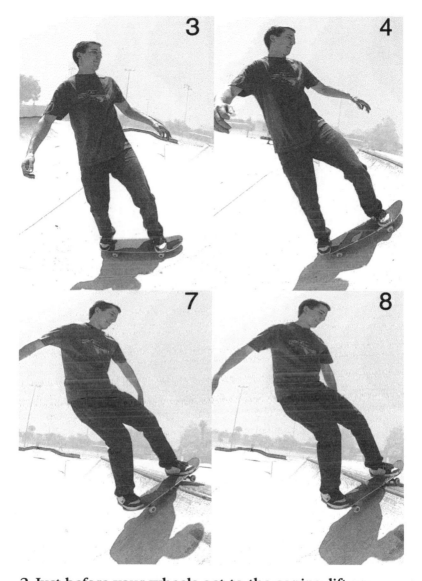

2. Just before your wheels get to the coping, lift up slightly by putting weight on your back foot.
3. As your front wheels lift above the coping and you reach the high point, push the front wheels down on the deck of the halfpipe.

4. It is important that your wheels do not go by the coping but rather go farther onto the deck of the half-pipe.

5. When your front wheels touch down on the deck, immediately rock back on the tail to lift your front

wheels. This action will take you back into the ramp.
6. Lean back into the ramp and keep your front wheels
lifted until you clear the coping. Then press your front
foot back down.
7. You want to have your weight over your back leg to
avoid slipping out when your front wheels go up on
the deck of the halfpipe and when you are coming
back in.

Key to remember: Most skaters just hang their front
wheels up on the coping and then unhook them
thinking they have done the trick. It takes confidence
to learn this trick the proper way and to not worry
about hanging up on the coping when you rock back
in.

3. Frontside 50-50 grind
1. Approach the coping at a very slight angle.
2. Your board should follow the transition up causing your front wheels to go into the air.
3. When your front wheels leave the ramp and your

back wheels are within a few inches of the coping, turn your shoulders so that they are parallel with the coping.

4. Your back truck should lock into 50-50. Aim your front truck so that it lands on the coping as well.

5. When you turn your back truck onto the coping, be sure to stand up over the coping rather than lean back into the ramp.

6. The faster you approach the coping, the faster and longer you will grind.

11 12

15 16

7. As your grind slows
down, put pressure on
your back foot and
slightly lift your front
truck.

8. As your front truck lifts,
turn your shoulders back
into the transition.

9. Be sure to put pressure
on your front foot so that
your front wheels touch
down on the ramp.

10. Lean forward as you
come back in.

The key to this trick is to stand up over the coping as
you turn into the 50-50 position.

4. Backside 50-50

1. Approach the coping at a slight angle.
2. Place your front foot over the top bolts on the front truck. Your back foot should be flat across the tail.
3. When you near the coping, lift your front truck so

that your back truck can close in on the coping.
4.When you feel the back truck touch the coping, turn
your front foot so that your front truck lands on the
coping. As your front and back trucks engage the
coping, stand up on your board so that you are over
the coping.

5. The faster you approach the coping, the faster and longer you will grind.

6. When you slow or stop, keep your balance and lift your back foot. Your front truck should lift and turn back into the ramp.

The key to this trick is to stand up while putting pressure on your heels in order to lock onto the coping and keep from slipping out.

5. Feeble stall

1. Approach the coping as if you were doing a rock to fakie.

2. When your front truck nears the coping, lift slightly by putting pressure on your back foot.

3. As your front truck lifts, turn your shoulders 45
degrees and push your back foot so that your back
truck stalls in feeble position.
4. When you are in feeble position, steady yourself and
put pressure on your back foot. This will lift your front

truck and turn you back into the transition.
5. Push your front wheels down on the ramp and lean forward to ensure balance.

Key to remember:
This trick is one of the easiest stalls on halfpipe
because you do not have to worry about hanging up. It
is also quite easy to get into the feeble position.

6. Frontside 5-0 grind

1. Before attempting this trick, it is important that you learn how to do frontside carves near the coping.
2. Drop in. Your front foot should be covering the bottom bolts of the front truck. Your back foot should

be placed flatly on the tail.

3.Approach the coping at a slight angle.

4.As you near the coping, your front truck should begin rising above the coping. As you feel the back truck near the coping, turn your front foot and

shoulders sharply so that your back is to the ramp.

5. The turning of your shoulders and front foot should cause your back truck to lock on the coping running parallel with it.

6. When your truck makes contact with the coping, place pressure on your back foot and hold your board in the 5-0 position.

7. Keep your weight centered over your back foot to ensure you don't slip out.

8. As you begin losing speed, turn your shoulder and feet in toward the ramp.

9. Drop your front foot and shoulder down into the transition for a safe ride away.

7. Backside 5-0

1. Approach the coping at a slight angle.
2. Have your front foot over the top bolts on your front truck. Your back foot should be flat across the tail.
3. When you near the coping, lift your front truck so

that your back truck can close in on the coping.
4. When your back truck hits the coping, shift your
weight to your back leg. This will keep your front truck
from touching down.

11   **12**

5. Put pressure on your back heel to bring the board up and level on the coping.

6. You should be grinding now or at least stalled in 5-0 position.

7. Begin turning your shoulders and front foot back into the ramp.

8. Transfer your weight to your front foot and bend your legs as the front wheels contact the ramp.

8. Frontside lipslide

1. Approach the coping at an angle.
2. When your front wheels are within six inches of the coping, snap an ollie toward the coping.
3. As your board lifts off the ramp, suck up your feet

and bend your legs. Rotate your shoulders so the board
will land in lipslide position.
4. Land with the middle of the board on the coping.
5. If you stall, you should approach the coping at a
bigger angle.

6. When you land on the coping, your front foot should be near the top bolts and partially on the nose.
7. As your slide slows, lean forward and transfer weight onto your front foot.

8. As your front wheels touch down on the ramp, push down on the nose slightly so that your back wheels lift without hanging up on the coping.

The secret to this trick is to sweep your shoulders and back foot around as you come up the transition so that you land in lipslide position.

9. Backside lipslide

1. Approach the coping at an angle.

2. As your front wheels lift above the coping, snap the tail on the ramp.

3. Swing your shoulders around so that your board

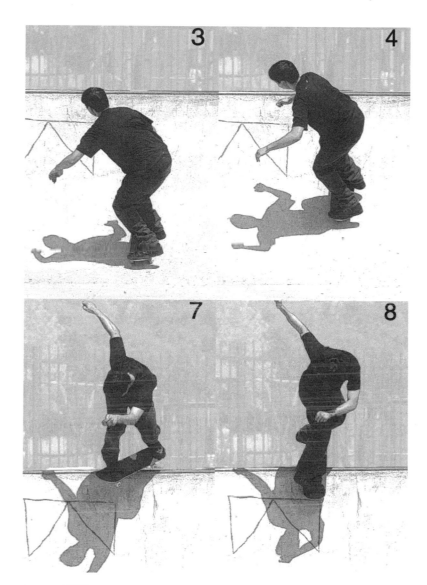

turns 180.

4. When you snap the tail and ascend the ramp, suck your legs into your chest.

5. Land with the middle of the board on the coping.

6. Extend your legs slightly as you slide.

7. When your slide slows, lean forward and transfer your weight to your front foot.

8. As your front wheels touch the coping, push the nose down slightly so that your back wheels lift and clear the coping. Roll back in.

The secret to this trick is to keep your balance as you turn and land on the coping. Looking into the ramp helps keep your balance.

10. Backside lipslide revert

1. Approach the coping at an angle.
2. As your front wheels lift above the coping, snap the tail on the ramp.
3. Swing your shoulders around so that your board

turns 180.

4. As you snap the tail and ascend the ramp, suck your legs into your chest.

5. You want to land with the middle of the board on the coping.

6. When you land on the coping, extend your legs slightly as you slide.

7. While your slide is coming to a stop, lean forward and transfer your weight to your front foot.

8. As your front wheels touch the ramp, push the nose down slightly, turn your shoulders and body and pivot on the front wheels so that you turn 180.

9. When you have completed the turn, push down on your back wheels and ride away fakie.

The secrets here are to pivot on the front wheels and to keep your weight leaning into the bottom of the ramp as you turn.

11. Fakie lip

This trick looks really cool and it's easy.

1. Approach the coping riding fakie.

2. As your back wheels near the coping, bend your knees and shove the board and your feet against the coping.

3. The quick shove or push of your feet should cause the wheels to bump the coping.

4. When you feel the back wheels bump the coping, suck your feet up.

5. The bump should cause your board to pop in the air.

Fakie lip

6. When your board pops up, push it down toward the coping so that the middle of your board lands on it.

7. Land in fakie position with your front foot near the nose and your back foot on the tail.

8. Place weight on the nose so that your back wheels lift. Lean forward and ride back in.

9. Weight on the nose and leaning forward should allow your back trucks to clear the coping.

The key is to be very loose when you bump your back wheels into the coping. And be sure to bring your legs up with the bump.

12. Half cab 50-50 stall

1. Approach the coping fakie.
2. When you feel your back wheels just about to touch the coping, put weight on your back foot and turn your board 45 degrees.

3. After turning, your back truck should end up on the coping.

4. Stand up on the board over the coping.

5. The front of your board should be in the air as you turn. When you lock your back truck, place your front

71

truck on the coping.

6. You should now be stalled on the coping in frontside 50-50 position.

7. Put weight on the tail and lift your front truck a bit, then turn back into the ramp.

8. Place weight on your front foot and push your front trucks down on the ramp.

The key is the timing of your turn.

13. Half cab fakie 5-0 stall

1. Approach the coping fakie.
2. As you feel your back wheels just about to touch the coping, put weight on your back foot and turn your board 45 degrees.

3. Your back truck should end up on the coping.
4. Stand up over the coping and put all your weight on your back foot so that your board is in the 5-0 position.
5. You should now be stalled on the coping in frontside 5-0 position.

6. Turn back into the ramp.
7. Place weight on your front foot and push your front truck down on the ramp.

The key is the timing of your turn as you ride fakie.

14. Half cab rock to fakie

1. Approach the coping riding fakie.
2. Your front foot should be across the bottom bolts on your front truck, and your back foot should be on the tail.

3. When your back wheels are about eight inches from the coping, lean back slightly.

4. You want to lean back to lift your front wheels but not enough for the tail to touch the ramp.

5. As your front wheels lift, turn your shoulders 180 degrees. Your board and body will follow.

6. After completing your 180, push your front wheels down on the deck of the halfpipe.

7. Lean back on the tail and lift your front wheels.

8. As your front wheels lift, lean back into the ramp. Push down on your front foot once you have cleared the coping.

The keys are to push your front wheels down on the deck and rock back in without hesitation.

15. Nose stall
1. This trick can be performed by ollie-ing into nose stall (which looks better) or by pressuring in.
2. When your front wheels are about a foot away from the coping, pop an ollie.

3. As you snap the tail and ollie, be sure to suck the tail up and push your front foot down to level the board.
4. When you ollie, move your board and weight toward the coping.

Nose stall

5. When the nose nears the coping, extend your front foot so that your board locks into nose stall position.

6. As you land with your nose on the coping, shift your weight to your front foot, which should be on the nose.

7. When you are in stall, push your back foot down and transfer your weight back into the ramp.

8. Push the back wheels down against the ramp so that you do not slip out.

The key is to ollie into the coping. This requires that you ollie before you reach the coping so that your weight is going into the lip.

16. Frontside tailslide

1. Approach the coping at a slight angle.
2. Your front foot should be placed slightly behind the bolts of your front truck, and your back foot should be placed in ollie position on the tail.

3. When your front wheels are eight inches away from the coping, snap the tail and ollie up toward the coping.

4. Turn your shoulders and body so that the tail is in place to land on the coping.

5. Push the tail and back wheels into the ramp so that you stall in tailslide position.

6. The angle and speed you approach the coping will determine how far you slide as well as the amount of pressure you'll need to hold the board in tailslide position.

7. When you slow down, put your weight on your front foot and lean back into the transition being sure to push your wheels to the ramp.

The keys are to turn your shoulders as you begin your ollie and to lean back on the tail as you near the coping.

17. Backside tailslide

1. Approach the coping at a slight angle.
2. Your front foot should be placed slightly behind the bolts of your front truck, and your back foot should be placed in ollie position on the tail.

3. When your front wheels are eight inches away from the coping, snap the tail and ollie up toward the coping.

4. As you ollie begin turning your shoulders and body so that the tail is in place to land on the coping.

5. Be sure to scoop the tail and ollie back into the coping.

6. As you ollie up toward the coping, push the tail and back wheels into the ramp so that you stall in tailslide position.

7. The angle and speed you approach the coping will determine how far you slide as well as the amount of pressure you'll need to hold the board in tailslide position.

8. As you slow down, put your weight on your front foot and lean back into the transition being sure to push your wheels to the ramp.

The keys are to scoop the tail around and to lean your body back so that you are able to stand up on your tailslide.

18. Backside carve

1.Approach the bowl corner with a fair amount of speed.

2.As you round the corner of the bowl, keep a straight line.

3. When you approach the first corner, suck your weight up by standing up. When you leave the corner, push all your weight down into your legs and push your body and board forward.

4. The feeling is the same as swinging, that is when you

were a kid on a swing set. You extended your legs as you went up and bent your legs as you came down, thus creating a pumping motion.

5. The key to carving in a bowl is to create a pumping motion as you go through each corner.

6. Keep all four wheels on the ramp at all times in order to maintain speed.

The keys are to stand up and to keep a straight line as you hit each corner.

Backside carve

19. Frontside carve

This trick is much the same as the backside carve.

1. Approach the bowl corner with a fair amount of speed.

2. As you round the corner of the bowl, keep a straight line.

3. When you approach the first corner, you want to suck your weight up by standing up, and as you leave, push all your weight down into your legs to push body and board forward.

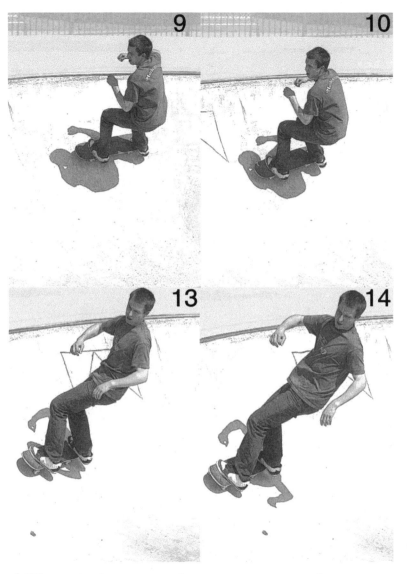

4. Like swinging on a swing, you pump your legs.
5. Creating pumping motions as you go through each corner is vital.
6. In order to keep your speed, keep all four wheels on the ramp at all times.

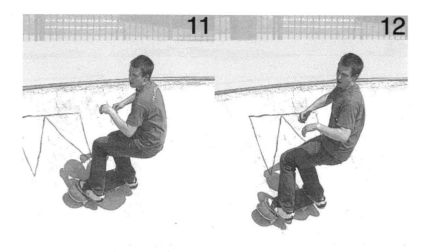

The key is to stand up going into the corners while keeping a straight line.

20. Backside 50-50 revert

1. Approach the coping at a slight angle.

2. Have your front foot over the top bolts on your front truck. Your back foot should be flat across the tail.

3. When you near the coping, lift your front truck so

that your back truck can hit the coping.

4.As you feel your back truck touch, turn your front foot so that your front truck lands on the coping. When your front and back trucks engage, stand up on your board so that you are over the coping.

5. Your approach speed will enable you to grind.
6. When you slow down, lift up your front truck slightly and turn your shoulders back into the ramp so that you are lined up riding fakie.

7. While you are still on your back truck, turn so that it disengages and your back wheels land on the ramp. Be sure to hold your front truck up until it clears the coping. 8. Lean over the back truck to center your balance as you come back in.

The key is leaning back over your back truck when you roll back in.

21. Frontside smith grind

1. Approach the coping with lots of speed.
2. Come in at a slight angle. As you near the coping, put pressure on the tail and lift your front wheels.

3. Push your back truck into the coping and into grind position.

4. When your back truck locks into grind position, push the nose down so that your front truck goes below the coping.

5. While pushing your front truck down, be sure to keep your weight centered on your back leg.
6. Your grind will depend on how much speed you approached the coping with and how locked into the smith position you are.

7. When your grind begins to slow, put slight pressure on the tail and turn back into the transition. Be sure to lean forward as you roll back in.

The secret to this trick is making the swooping push in order to get your back truck into the smith position.

22. Backside smith grind

1.Approach the coping with speed and at a slight angle.

2.As your front wheels near the coping, make a large carving turn so that your front truck turns over and

past the coping and your back truck hits it.
3. When you feel your back truck nearing the coping, give your board a push so that your back truck hits with force.
4. When your back truck hits the coping, slam it into

grind by pushing your weight over and into the coping. Your front leg should be holding the front part of your board in smith grind position.

5. When you feel the board slowing, simply turn your board into the ramp, transfer your weight to your front wheels and roll away.

The keys are the carving turn into the coping and pushing your back truck hard into the coping in order to create the grind.

11 12

13 14

1 **2**

5 **6**

23. Pivot fakie

1. Approach the coping as if you were going to do a backside 50-50 stall.

2. As you ride up to the coping, press down slightly on the tail and lift your front wheels.

3. As your back wheels approach the coping, push your back wheels up and turn or pivot so that your back truck locks into a stall on the coping.

4. Keep your weight against the tail and hold your front foot up as it rests over the top bolts.

9   10

5. Lean back into the ramp and turn your front foot back so that your board is straight again.

6. Roll backward into the ramp. Be sure to keep your front wheels up so they do not hang up on the coping when you ride back in.

7. Stay low and keep your balance over the back truck so that you do not slip out.

8. As you ride back in and your front truck clears the coping, push down to make contact with the ramp.

The keys are to keep your balance when you ride back in and to be confident when you lean back into the ramp.

11
12

13
14

24. Blunt to fakie

1. Approach the coping straight on. Place your front foot over the top set of bolts and your back foot flat across the tail.

2. When your front wheels near the coping, lift slightly

and allow your back wheels to ride up to the coping.
3. As your back wheels near the coping, push your back
foot up slightly so that your back wheels ride over the
coping.
4. Push firmly against the coping. You should be in

blunt position.

5. As soon as your board gets in blunt position, push down very slightly on your front foot and snap the tail back against the ramp.

6. Bring your front foot back and hop backward into the ramp.

7. When you feel your back wheels near the coping, push your back foot against the ramp so that your wheels touch. When you feel your front truck has cleared the coping, push your front wheels down as well.

8. Bend your legs as you hop back into the ramp.

The key to this trick is to snap out of the blunt as soon as you get into it. Hesitation will cause you to lose momentum and freeze up.

25. Blunt to rock to fakie

1. Approach the coping straight on. Place your front foot over the top set of bolts and your back foot flat across the tail.

2. As your front wheels near the coping, lift them

slightly and allow your back wheels to ride up the rest of the transition.

3.As your back wheels approach the coping, push your back foot up slightly so that your back wheels ride over the coping.

4. Push firmly against the coping. You should now be in the blunt position.

5. As soon as your board gets in blunt position, push down very slightly on your front foot and snap the tail back against the ramp.

6. As you snap the tail, bring your front foot back, hop backward and back into the ramp.

7. As you feel your back wheels clear the coping, level out the board and push your front wheels down so that you land in fakie position.

8. When your front wheels touch down on the deck of the ramp, rock back into the ramp by pushing down on the tail and lifting your front truck up.

9. When your front truck has lifted above the coping and you are riding back in, push your front truck down so that you are able to ride away.

The key is to push the nose down when you snap out of the blunt so that you level out.

26. Frontside noseblunt

1. Approach the coping with speed and at a slight angle.

2. As your front wheels near the coping, snap the tail and begin to slide your front foot up the board as you

would for an ollie.
3. When you reach the highest point of the ollie, turn your shoulders, body and feet 180 degrees.
4. Aim the nose of your board for the coping.
5. As you come down, extend your front leg so that the

nose locks into noseblunt position.

6. Your back leg should be bent while your front foot extends to hold the slide.

7. As you land in the noseblunt position, your front foot should be pushing the board so that you slide.

8. Now comes the difficult part. Be sure to slide straight across the coping so that you are in line to come back in.

9. When you begin to slow, push down quickly with your front foot and create a pop. Push back with your back foot so that the board does a nollie and your front truck clears the coping.

10. Pop hard enough to get your front wheels back into the ramp. Push your weight down over your front wheels and your back foot, once your wheels have cleared the coping.

The secret to this trick is to pop back into the ramp while you are still sliding so that you have momentum to come back in.

27. Frontside hurricane

1. Approach the coping backside at a slight angle.
2. Ride up as if you were going to do a backside 50-50.
3. When your front truck nears the coping, turn your board so that you are doing a frontside 180 turn.

4. As you turn, tilt the board back a bit and slam your back truck into the coping.
5. Your weight should be against the back truck.
6. As you slow down on your grind, turn back 180 and put your front wheels back into the transition.

9 10 13 14

The key is slamming your back wheels into the coping so that you lock into hurricane grind.

11   **12**

28. K grind fakie

1. Approach the coping at a slight angle.
2. As you near the coping with your front truck, snap an ollie.
3. When the tail hits the ramp, drag your front foot up

on the board and aim the nose for the coping.
4. Your front truck should hit the coping. When it hits, push your weight down on your front truck and hold your board in K grind position.
5. As your grind begins to slow, turn your board so that you are facing fakie into the ramp.

6. When your board lines up to ride back in fakie, push down on your back foot.

7. Be sure to lean back into the ramp as you push down.

The keys to this trick are to ollie and aim the nose for the coping. Also be sure to lean back into the ramp to ensure a successful ride away.

29. Nosegrind

1. Approach the coping at an angle, as if you were going for a 50-50.
2. When your front truck is nearing the coping, snap the tail against the ramp and ollie.

3. Drag your front foot up the board and aim the nose for the coping.

4. When your front truck is over the coping, extend your front leg so that you land in nosegrind position.

5. You should be grinding.

9

6. When you begin to slow down, swing your back leg around over the deck of the ramp.
7. Lean back into the ramp and keep your weight over your front leg.
8. When your back truck has cleared the coping, push your back leg down so that all four wheels are on the ramp.

The key to this trick is coming back into the ramp. It requires balance as you lean forward on your way back into the ramp.

30. Ollie

1. Begin learning this trick with minimal speed.
2. As you ride up the transition, pop an ollie.
3. Snap the tail and drag your front foot up.
4. As you ascend, push your front foot down slightly so

that your board levels out in the air.
5. When you come down, make sure both sets of wheels land at the same time. Or have your front wheels land a split second before your back wheels.

6. As you land on the ramp, be sure to keep your knees bent and your weight over your back foot a bit so that you don't slip out.

The key to this trick is to push down slightly on your front foot so that your board levels out in the air.

11   12

31. Frontside ollie

1. Approach the transition with enough speed to get your board above the coping. Make sure you do not go too fast and lose control.
2. Approach the coping at a slight angle.

3. Before your front wheels go above the coping, snap an ollie.

4. As you snap the tail, turn your shoulders so that your body and board turn back into the ramp.

5. While turning keep your knees bent so that your board stays with your feet.

6. After you complete your turn, lean your front shoulder back into the ramp.
7. Extend your legs to absorb impact.

The key to learning this trick is to practice near the bottom of the ramp doing small airs. You will get the feel of taking off and landing in the transition of the ramp.

32. Kickflip

1. Start learning with minimal speed.
2. As you ride up the transition, have your front foot in the kickflip position.
3. Snap the tail and drag your front foot up and across

the board.

4. As you ascend, keep your feet up so that your board can flip.

5. When the board has flipped the right amount, extend your legs to stop its flipping.

9　　　　　　10

13　　　　　　14

11   12

6. Push your front foot down slightly so that your board levels out in the air.

7. When you come down, make sure that both wheels land at the same time. Or have your front wheels land a split second before your back wheels.

8. As you land on the ramp, keep your knees bent and your weight over your back foot a bit so you don't slip out.

The keys are to do a nice kickflip, suck your legs up as the board flips and extend them once the board is nearing the end of the flip.

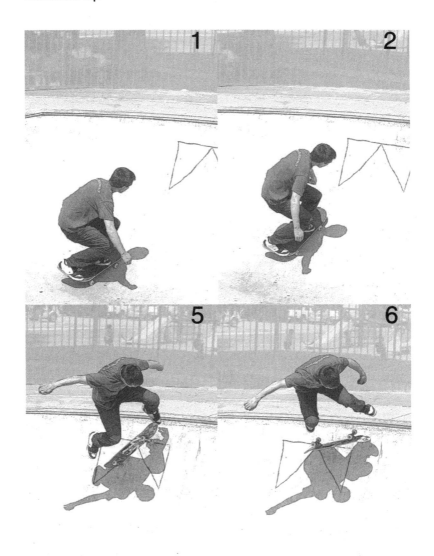

33. Backside flip
1. Approach the coping at a slight angle.
2. When you snap the tail will determine how high you go. Here the front wheels are about 10 inches from the coping.

3. Your front foot should be at a 45 degree angle and your toes a little past the center line of your board. Your back foot should be in the middle of the tail.
4. When you're about 10 inches from the coping, snap the tail and flick your front foot out and around so that

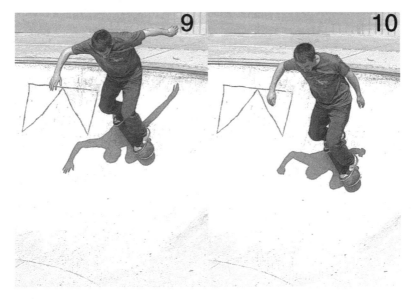

your board flips and turns 180.

5. Turn your shoulders and body as you flick the board around.

6. When you feel the board complete the flick, lean forward into the ramp and put your feet down.

7. As you land, bend your knees and keep your balance by leaning forward.

The key is flicking your foot so that your board kickflips 180.

34. Frontside flip
1. Approach the coping with your front foot slightly below the front truck in kickflip position.
2. When your front truck nears the coping, snap the tail as you would for a frontside 180.

3. As you snap the tail, rotate your shoulders and kick your front foot straight off the side of the nose and around as you would for a frontside flip. Be sure to suck your legs up as you kick and rotate.
4. When you have turned 90 degrees, you should feel

that the board is near its flip and under your feet.
5. Look down to see if the board has flipped correctly and is ready to land.
6. Extend your legs as you finish the 180 rotation so that your board touches down at the same time.
7. Bend your knees to ensure a safe ride away.

The key to this trick is flipping the board by the time you get 90. The rest of the turn will come naturally.

35. Kickflip nosestall

1. Approach the coping straight on.
2. Your front foot should be behind the bolts and in kickflip position.
3. When your front truck is about six inches from the

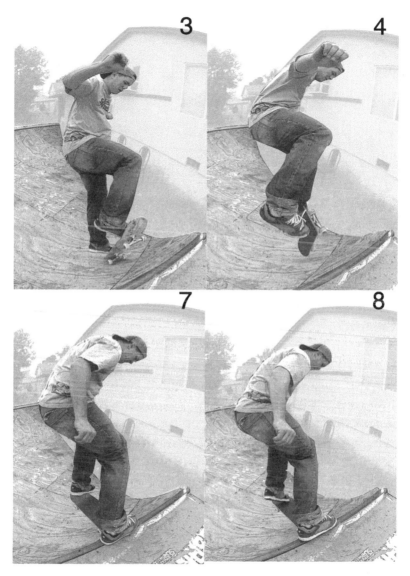

coping, snap the tail as you would for an ollie. Flick
your front foot up and to the side of the board causing
it to kickflip up.
4. When you feel the nose has gone past the coping,
place your front foot on the board and begin to push

down slightly so that your back truck levels out with the front.

5. As your board is leveling out, push your front foot down so that the nose lands on the coping.

6. As you are kickflipping, try to land with your front foot on the nose.

7. Aim the nose toward the coping and land with your weight over the nose of your board.

8. When you land in nose stall position, push down on your back foot so that you ride back into the ramp. Transfer your weight to your back leg to avoid slipping out.

The key is to level out your kickflip in the air so that you can land in nose stall position.

Resources / Evan's picks

DC Shoe Co USA
DC Shoes has been around for quite some time and has some of the best riders in the world. Their Web site hosts recent skateboard news as well as some awesome skateboard footage.
www.dcshoecousa.com

Metro Clothes
Evan has started his own clothing company called Metro Clothes. Check out the Web site and buy some shirts off it.
www.metrofoundation.net

Skateboard Village
Skateboard Village is a Web site dedicated to posting chat rooms for skateboarders and snowboarders. Skateboarders can post their glory shots for the world to see.
www.skateboardvillage.com

Slap Magazine
Slap Magazine is another skateboard magazine like *Transworld* and *Thrasher*. It can be found in skateshops and convenience stores.
www.slapmagazine.com

Thrasher Magazine
Thrasher Magazine features Northern California skateboarding and special articles devoted to both punk and hip-hop music. This magazine is sold at most skateshops and convenience stores.
www.thrashermagazine.com

Transworld Skateboarding Magazine
This is a great magazine for those wanting to stay current with skateboarding news, tricks and culture. It's available at almost every book store and convenience store.
www.skateboarding.com

United Riders Clothing
United Clothing is a skateboard clothing company that sponsors many top skateboarders. Check out there Web site and watch mayhem and skateboard footage www.united-riders.com

Zero Skateboards
Zero skateboards is home to some of the best upcoming amateurs and pros. The Web site has interviews with riders, pictures and footage.
www.zeroskate.com

Zion Skateboards
Zion Skateboards is a skateboard company based in Vancouver, B.C., Canada. Evan currently rides for them and recommends their skateboards because of the quality and price. Check out there Web site and watch footage of Evan.
www.zionskate.com

Resources / comprehensive

For a quick fix go to **www.skateboarding.com** — an informative (but not the only) portal into the skateboarding galaxy.

Books
Discovered on **amazon.com** and **barnesandnoble.com**.

Baccigaluppi, John. *Declaration of Independents*. San Francisco, California: Chronicle Books, 2001.

Bermudez, Ben. *Skate! The Mongo's Guide to Skateboarding*. New York, New York: Cheapskate Press, 2001.

Borden, Ian. *Skateboarding, Space and the City*. New York, New York: Berg, 2001.

Brooke, Michael. *The Concrete Wave: The History of Skateboarding*. Toronto, Ontario: Warwick Publishing, 1999.

Burke, L.M. *Skateboarding! Surf the Pavement*. New York, New York: Rosen Publishing Group, Inc., 1999.

Davis, James. *Skateboard Roadmap*. England: Carlton Books Limited, 1999.

Gould, Marilyn. *Skateboarding*. Mankato, Minnesota: Capstone Press, 1991.

Gutman, Bill. *Skateboarding: To the Extreme*. New York, New York: Tom Doherty Associates, Inc., 1997.

Hawk, Tony. *Hawk*. New York, New York: Regan Books, 2001.

Powell, Ben. *Extreme Sports: Skateboarding*. Hauppauge, New York: Barron's Educational Series, Inc., 1999.

Riggins, Edward. *Ramp Plans*. San Francisco, California: High Speed Productions, 2000.

Ryan, Pat. *Extreme Skateboarding*. Mankato, Minnesota: Capstone Press, 1998.

Shoemaker, Joel. *Skateboarding Streetstyle*. Mankato, Minnesota: Capstone Press, 1995.

Thrasher. *Insane Terrain*. New York, New York: Universe Publishing, 2001.

Camps
Donny Barley Skate Camp
1747 West Main Road
Middletown, Rhode Island
02842
401-848-8078

Lake Owen
HC 60 Box 60
Cable, Wisconsin 54821
715-798-3785

Magdalena Ecke Family YMCA
200 Saxony Road
Encinitas, California 92023-0907
760-942-9622

Mission Valley YMCA
5505 Friars Road
San Diego, California 92110
619-298-3576

Skatelab
Steve Badillo Skate Camp
4226 Valley Fair Street
Simi Valley, California 93063
805-578-0040
vtaskate@aol.com

Snow Valley
PO Box 2337
Running Springs, California 92382
909-867-2751

Visalia YMCA
Sequoia Lake, California
211 West Tulare Avenue
Visalia, California 93277
559-627-0700

Woodward Camp
Box 93
Route 45
Woodward, Pennsylvania 16882
814-349-5633

Young Life Skate Camp
Hope, British Columbia, Canada
604-807-3718

Magazines

Big Brother
www.bigbrothermagazine.com

Skateboarder
Surfer Publications
PO Box 1028
Dana Point, California 92629

Thrasher
High Speed Productions
1303 Underwood Avenue
San Francisco, California 94124
415-822-3083
www.thrashermagazine.com

Transworld Skateboarding
353 Airport Road
Oceanside, California 92054
760-722-7777
www.skateboarding.com

Museums

Huntington Beach International
Skate and Surf Museum
411 Olive Street
Huntington Beach, California
714-960-3483

Skatelab
4226 Valley Fair
Simi Valley, California
805-578-0040
www.skatelab.com

Skatopia
34961 Hutton Road
Rutland, Ohio 45775
740-742-1110

Organizations, movers, shakers . . .
Action Sports Retailer
Organizer of the Action Sports
Retailer Trade Expos
949-376-8144
www.asrbiz.com

California Amateur Skateboard
League (CASL) and PSL
Amateur and professional
contest organizer
909-883-6176
Fax 909-883-8036

The Canadian Cup
416-960-2222

Extreme Downhill International
1666 Garnet Avenue #308
San Diego, California 92109
619-272-3095

International Association of
Skateboard Companies (IASC)
PO Box 37
Santa Barbara, California 93116
805-683-5676
Fax 805-967-7537
iascsk8@aol.com
www.skateboardiasc.org

International Network
for Flatland Freestyle
Skateboarding
Abbedissavagen 15
746 95 Balsta, Sweden

KC Projects
Canadian amateur contest
organizer
514-806-7838
kc_projects@aol.com
5148067838@fido.ca

National Amateur Skateboard
Championships
Damn Am Series
National amateur contest
organizer
813-621-6793
www.skateparkoftampa.com
www.nascseries.com

National Skateboarders
Association of Australia (NSAA)
Amateur and professional
contest organizers
61-2-9878-3876
www.skateboard.asn.au

The Next Cup
Southern California amateur
contest organizer
858-874-4970 ext. 114 or 129
www.thenextcup.com

Real Amateur Skateboarding
Amateur contest organizer
619-501-1341
realamateurskateboarding
@hotmail.com

Skateboarding Association of
America
Amateur contest organizer
727-523-0875
www.skateboardassn.org

Skatepark Association of the USA (SPAUSA)
Resource for skate park planning/operating
310-823-9228
www.spausa.org

Southwest Sizzler
Southwestern amateur contest organizer
918-638-6492

Surf Expo
East Coast trade show
800-947-SURF
www.surfexpo.com

United Skateboarding Association (USA)
Skate event organizer and action sport marketing/promotions
732-432-5400
ext. 2168 and 2169
www.unitedskate.com

Vans Shoes
Organizer of the Triple Crown skate events
562-565-8267
www.vans.com

World Cup Skateboarding
Organizer of some of skating's largest events
530-888-0596
Fax 530-888-0296
danielle@wcsk8.com
www.wcsk8.com

Zeal Skateboarding Association
Southern California amateur contest organizer
909-265-3420
www.zealsk8.com

Public skate parks / information about building and starting up

Consolidated Skateboards
(see *The Plan*)
www.consolidatedskateboard.com

International Association of Skateboard Companies (IASC)
PO Box 37
Santa Barbara, California 93116
805-683-5676
Fax 805-967-7537
iascsk8@aol.com
www.skateboardiasc.org

Skatepark Association of the USA (SPAUSA)
310-823-9228
www.spausa.org

www.skatepark.org

Public skate park designers / builders

Airspeed Skateparks LLC
2006 Highway 101 #154
Florence, Oregon 97439
503-791-4674
airspeed@airspeedskateparks.com
www.airspeedskateparks.com

171

CA Skateparks, Design/Build
and General Contracting
273 North Benson Avenue
Upland, California 91786
562-208-4646
www.skatedesign.com

Dreamland Skateparks,
Grindline, Inc.
4056 23rd Avenue SW
Seattle, Washington 98106
206-933-7915
www.grindline.com

Ramptech
www.ramptech.com

SITE Design Group, Inc.
414 South Mill Avenue,
Suite 210
Tempe, Arizona 85281
480-894-6797
Fax 480-894-6792
mm@sitedesigngroup.com
www.sitedesigngroup.com

Spectrum Skatepark
Creations, Ltd.
M/A 2856 Clifftop Lane
Whistler, B.C.
V0N 1B2 Canada
250-238-0140
design@spectrum-sk8.com
www.spectrum-sk8.com

Team Pain
864 Gazelle Trail
Winter Springs, Florida 32708
407-695-8215
tim@teampain.com
www.teampain.com

John Woodstock Designs
561-743-5963
johnwoodstock@msn.com
www.woodstockskateparks.com

**Shops / skate parks
finding one close to you**
Two (among quite a few) that
will help:
www.skateboarding.com
www.skateboards.org

**Television
ESPN**
X Games
espn.go.com/extreme

NBC
Gravity Games
www.gravitygames.com

Web sites
www.board-trac.com
Market researchers for skateboarding industry.

www.bigbrother.com
A comprehensive site by *Big
Brother* magazine.

www.exploratorium.edu/
skateboarding
Glossary, scientific explanations
and equipment for skating.

www.interlog.com/~mbrooke/
skategeezer.html
International Longboarder
magazine.

www.ncdsa.com
Northern California Downhill
Skateboarding Association.

www.skateboardiasc.org
International Association of
Skateboard Companies (IASC) is
one of the leading advocates of
skateboarding progress and pro-
vides a wealth of information.

www.skateboard.com
Chat and messages.

www.skateboarding.com
Every skater's site by
Transworld Skateboarding
magazine.

www.skateboards.org
Find parks, shops and
companies.

www.skatelab.com
One of Los Angeles area's
largest indoor parks and world's
largest skateboard museum.

www.skater.net
Skate parks and ramp plans.

www.smithgrind.com
Skate news wire.

www.switchmagazine.com
*Switch Skateboarding
Magazine.*

www.thrashermagazine.com
A comprehensive site by
Thrasher magazine.

Videos / Instructional

411 Video Productions. *The
First Step.*

411 Video Productions. *The
Next Step.*

Hawk, Tony. *Tony Hawk's Trick
Tips Volume I: Skateboarding
Basics.* 900 Films, 2001.

Hawk, Tony. *Tony Hawk's Trick
Tips Volume II: Essentials of
Street.* 900 Films, 2001.

Thrasher Magazine. *How to
Skateboard.* San Francisco,
California: High Speed
Productions, Inc., 1995.

Thrasher Magazine. *How to
Skateboard Better.* San
Francisco, California: High
Speed Productions, Inc., 1997.

Transworld Skateboarding.
Starting Point. Oceanside,
California, 1997.

Transworld Skateboarding. *Trick
Tips with Wily Santos.*
Oceanside, California, 1998.

Transworld Skateboarding.
Starting Point Number Two.
Oceanside, California, 1999.

Index

More skate guides from Tracks

Skateboarder's Start-Up:
A Beginner's Guide to Skateboarding
$11.95
An essential start-up guide.

Skateboarding: New Levels
Tricks and Tips for Serious Riders
$12.95
Intermediate and advanced skating.

Skateboarding: Book of Tricks
$12.95
A look at old-school and new-school skateboarding.

Street Skateboarding: Endless Grinds and Slides
$12.95
Curb tricks galore.

Street Skateboarding: Flip Tricks
$12.95
Nothing but flips!

Our skate guides are the most popular skate instructional books on the globe because they're inexpensive and contain hundreds of sequential images to explain the tricks you should know. Available at all major bookstores and booksellers on the Internet.

About the author

Evan Goodfellow is a lifelong skater and skateboard instructor. He is the author of *Street Skateboarding: Endless Grinds and Slides* and *Street Skateboarding: Flip Tricks*. Evan has also appeared in eight skate videos.

His sponsors have included Vans Shoes, Ambiguous Clothing, Zion Skateboards and Ninetimes Boardshop. He earned a master's degree in education from Biola University, La Mirada, California in 2004.

Evan is starting up a clothing company with a few friends. Check it out. www.metrofoundation.net.